T0210213

TURNING TO WALLPAPER

poems & art by

HEIDI WONG

central
avenue
PUBLISHING

2021

Published by Central Avenue Publishing, an imprint of Central Avenue Marketing Ltd.
www.centralavenuepublishing.com

TURNING TO WALLPAPER: POEMS & ART

Trade Paper: 978-1-77168-246-6
Ebook: 978-1-77168-247-3

Printed in United States of America

1. POETRY / Women Authors   2. POETRY / Asian American

10 9 8 7 6 5 4 3 2 1

This too is true: stories can save us.

— Tim O'Brien

2020

you lose seeing the snow melt one last time.
lose your corner room in the gray cement building,

lose friends, lose childhood, lose new york, lose
him. you witness distance spreading

beyond distance. you learn
distance becomes distance by feeding

on your ability to see it. all it takes is one person
to give up. he takes the jewels of your irises

and says *i don't care.* you try to starve,
but the dead brother inside your stomach

demands food. the grief
just won't cut it.

isolation wraps around your neck like a lover.
would you leave, even if you could? where would you

go? two weeks later you are so yourself
it's frightening. hope sinks

into your skin like light. at night,
sometimes, only sometimes, like a blade

scraping away gemstone fantasies. would you
leave, even if you could? where would you

go? your home
that was never your home bursts

into flame and you are at the beach for daddy's birthday,
pretending your friends aren't losing their fingers to gunfire.

you say *be careful* when you mean
i love you.

you say *when they bring out the gas start running* when you mean
i love you. you say *don't be a hero* when you mean

i can't lose you
too.

a man dies on camera. and across the pacific
an orchestra of coarse, frozen throats begins to remember

it still has a voice to speak with. a voice
stretching to silver lakes, casting the shape of the future.

maybe heaven births itself
from the mouths that mourn your absence.

maybe death is the only commonality
mankind can agree on.

a black man is murdered on camera.
and one of the officers wears your uncle's face

as he boards the flight and does not return
till two years after nana gets lowered

into our motherland. he comforts himself
in a white man's country, thinking

she wouldn't have remembered me anyway.
the last thing nana called for was her son.

a girl who looks like you,
could have been you, is

you, bleeds in the street. they call her *dirty chinese*,
and it's the first time in seven years you wished

you were white. your western home
threatens your eastern home

and you go to sleep wondering,
if you had to gouge one of your eyes out,

which would you choose? pray
for the rustle of autumn in clinton.

but normal is a hand with missing fingers,
the new family that never learned your name.

you know you can, someday might even,
for real this time, unashamed this time,

without fear this time,
love. but what good is that now?

HOW MANY CALORIES ARE IN A BOTTLE OF ORANGE JUICE?

once, i am undone by the milky surface of auntie's feeding tube.
the cancer ate the fat off her bones. the rest of her,
too. in my country, food is love. but it is also
guilt. the cashier at the supermarket across the street
says *i don't know how many calories are in a bottle of orange juice.*
to think, the act of stalking prey
is one part sustenance and all parts hunt. once,
i dream of being the main character—a skinny white girl
who finds love by saying *yes.* once,
i lock myself in the storage closet to avoid
the first day of swim class. once,
i learn there is a finite number of attributes
one can be referring to when saying *you are pretty,*
just not in the conventional way. once,
i lose my voice. then,
clumps of hair that clog the shower drain. but never any weight.
i tell myself it's because i am not brave enough
to be anorexic. the american boy who said *you are too fat for me*
apologizes. i forgive him the way my body
forgives me. that night,
the marks on my thighs crack into lightning.
i curl into bed and strum my ribs like an old violin. home
tastes like blue cherry candy and half healed wrists. home
is anywhere i no longer feel guilty. to claim
i love myself, always,
would imply a love that ignores its history. before
auntie died, she paid thousands for a vial of cough syrup
that promised to shrink the tumor. when her ashes mixed
into the ocean, the waves smelled of medicine
and magic. there was nothing

abnormal to van gogh's hunger
for yellow paint. in the absence
of a cure, peace is its imitation.

TO THE GODS WHO DO NOTHING

exit chronos

the tumor melts into my rib cage, my brother's heart
begins again. the sheets where the bad thing happened
unstain themselves, the scent of bleach
walks out of my sophomore dorm room.
stability chokes the bluebird in my skull
who always begs to seek another land.
this time, enough feels enough.

grandma remembers the name she gave me,
auntie's hair in the kitchen sink rises
to meet her scalp. my family in the ground
cleans the dirt off their faces and comes home.
i save the bent-neck boy, the pinkwater
in my mother's bathtub retreats into my forearm,
and i never become a poet.

exit forseti

i spoke to god, first, under water,
when i was sixteen. rose-painted bathwater,
air conditioning all the way down. my arms,
raised upwards like knives, a pair of open doorways
begging to seek another land.
yet she only watched, with an aura of tranquil nothingness,
as the drowning became my baptism.

i spoke to her again when auntie's chest burst
into a thousand suns, so bright

it blinded everyone around her.
she stopped playing piano, stopped dancing,
stopped reading me stories.

and when we made the left turn an hour before my flight to new york,
god was there too, doused in tigereye dusk.
my uncle called mama from inside the hospice to say
take her away. don't let her remember me
like this. two weeks later he was in the ocean,
and my twin life was beginning on the other side of it.
faith says this is how he tried to reach me,
each glimmer of him swimming tirelessly
towards the new continent i called home.

god, too, followed me to new york. to the room
that became a glen, a glen
that became my skin. when a man pinned my eyes to his ceiling,
licked the wounds, filled my bones with leeches.
"Come, let us go, and make thy father blind."
but i could not make my father blind. could not make him fall
to his knees and plead—*lay your hands on her, make her well,*
let her live.

the next morning, god
watched me clean the evidence with bleach. *soak twice,*
don't let the neighbors see. if you want to live,
live.

exit eirene

forgiveness was foreign before the sparrow boy
found dangling from his neck, lavendered
before he hit the ground. i led his ghost

to auntie, to uncle, to grandma, to grandpa, to henry,
but the grave of my body was full;
they could not live there anymore.

love was an eternal cloud before i lost my legs in the woods.
in dreams, i return there. i caress what i abandoned,
what abandoned me, what had to be
abandoned, then leave it to die.

had he not damned me to be a monster,
how could medusa cut off the head of theseus
and wear his eyes around her neck like a love poem?

had someone, anyone, found me there,
had they replaced *liar* with jupiter's mercy—
"We will mourn with thee. O, could our mourning ease thy misery"—
how much longer would a child of lilith
bleed the blood of eve?

would i be so sure of this body, had it not been shaped
by the lack of salvation?

god is a girl who leans against your desk
as you peel betrayal off your skin.
her presence, a voice that says
these are the wounds that must happen to you.

god is a mirror above the water
looking down with your eyes;
if you want to live, live.

enter aion

on the last night i spent in new york,
i went ice skating alone. when it got dark,
i traced the oculus of the lake, backlit
by the onyx sky that sculpted me into myself,
and saw her beneath the ice, the ice,
not unlike a teenage scar,
as if she were trying to reach for something.

but i just stood there,
watching the water invade her features,
allowing her the space
to forgive her becoming.

LAVINIA DOES NOT DIE AND INSTEAD BECOMES A POET

> Tumble me into some loathsome pit
> Where never man's eye may behold my body.
>
> —William Shakespeare, *Titus Andronicus*

this body is not the same body that walked out of the forest.
a limbless deer, a house without windows. i may have cried, even.
but no witnesses recall those tears, so there might as well have been none.

the eastern gods led me home, the western gods followed.
then, together, they hung themselves by my front porch
as i cleaned my severed wrists and sang,
"Fair Philomela, why, she but lost her tongue."

so what else is left but to speak without a tongue,
to grip the edge of poetry like a blood basin
until i grow ghost hands?

i haven't been in milbank since. that wall-less glen
where each gust of wind becomes the breath of a silent audience,
where every tree sprouts eyes. my new bones
do not want me there.

they say a woman should never survive her shame.
because any woman who does
will force her stomach to swell with words

and bleed into the kirkland sky
until the tongues of her ghost hands haunt these woods,
long after her body forgets.

THE HOUSE

my dead aunt puts her famous rosemary chicken in the oven,
her worms eyeing my ripened neck.
she smiles in her brown fur coat like she did in 2008.
i remember calling her beautiful
after the chemicals peeled the woman off her bones.

that weekend, i tell the stranger in the bathroom *don't worry.*
i am a house. a pile of cracked walnuts on the table.
miniature herbs by the windowsill left to writhe with thirst.
two fingers inside the mason jar,
to plant the piece of rosemary deeper into my throat.

THE ONLY CHILD

my parents will die before me
and i will scatter them into the south china sea
watch their rigidness soften with the waves
because my mother is claustrophobic and can't sleep
in that dark place underground and my father
would want to be with her
i won't move the coffeemaker for ten years
won't put away their winter shoes from the doorway
scrub the wine stains off the tablecloth
i will kiss their opal hands
feel my heart expand like a sponge full of blood
lie in the furnace between their lavendered bodies
like i used to when the nightmares were bad
and the cousin who never learned my name will wait outside
preaching to every god we saw in ourselves
western gods and asian gods the same ones
who couldn't stop her mother's cancer from growing
after a few hours i will crawl out like a newborn
go back to the home that is not a home
talk to my dead brother the way i spoke to god in middle school
to stop the cancer from growing
tell him it's his turn to be the only child
to know how they like their coffee made
their favorite brand of winter shoes
and we will sit in the house that is now one room
reminding each other with the voice i stole from him in 1998
how a child is nothing but an organ
that when carved from the body
can choose to survive on its own

TO THE THREE SUITCASES I LEFT IN A STORAGE UNIT IN NEW YORK

i don't regret any of it. not the fireworks in brooklyn,
the church outside my bolted windows, the ochre stains

in the communal shower. not the broken washer,
the slides with the side part ripped off, the two dollar coffee

from the bakery on tenth street. not the friends
who knew it all except why, why,

why, not the youth spinning dizzy with gasoline eyes,
not the streetlamps churning to angels.

not the men, the town. not even the house
we built with snow water.

but who do i pray to now? my sanctuary is a mouth
full of blood.

the avenues gawk at my foreignness.
even the shame can't bleach my skin

white. america,
america, you are the lover who never wanted me.

and i am more afraid than i am grieving.
so maybe there's something triumphant

about heartbreak, too. the way it opens,
the way it spills. somewhere,

another sunset dampens the evening
with fresh pollen yellow. somewhere,

children who look like me lie
in sparkling snow. their laughter,

the same voice i once swore was useless.
let me find you, let me find you.

AN OBSERVATION OF SHADOWS

i imagine we end like this. outside
the church, a photo

raised to the sun. glossy,
graying inwards, frozen in the posture

of the last time we understood
each other. remembrance

is, by itself, a sickness.
the rind of a fruit drying,

only to preserve its scent. there are many
names for *i no longer remember*

the person i was when i allowed you
to make me happy. one of which is

silence. i imagine
we end like this.

a photo returned to my blue coat.
an evening of watching

the shadows on the church shift
without hesitation, resolute and powerless

in each movement. the quiet proof
of how the same body, always,

without fail, bends
to accommodate the hour.

HOW I BECAME AN ATHEIST

even my dog
who once worshipped
its owner's presence
knew to stop
shaking the metal fence
around my front yard
the day it noticed
i no longer had anything left
to feed it

LOVE LETTER FROM THE RAZOR BLADE TAPED TO THE BACK OF MY IPOD FROM MIDDLE SCHOOL

you stepped out of the bathtub
the way you crawled out of milbank. handless,
tongueless, two bodied, and
stillborn. you say *at least the water was peaceful.* as if
his shadow did not fill your lungs. as if,
three years later, you aren't coughing up mouthfuls of memory
in strangers' bathrooms. you
stepped out. handless,
tongueless, two bodied, and
stillborn. still,
the stillborn spoke without a tongue
and made men afraid. still,
the stillborn scratched color into her skin until her skin
blushed like summer
again. now
you are more alive than the living, the living
who do not know what it means
to die worse deaths than your real death and still
not die. to crawl
out, naked,
fetal, quivering from the pinkwater, and still
rename the drowning as
baptism. still
rename the drowning as
holy. as an ode to everything
that tried to push you out of your body
and failed.

3 IN 4

when you tell your daughter
to have fun and carry pepper spray
in the same breath. when she runs
into your arms, earlobe torn, skirt ripped,
wanting to die. when you witness
the blush of her cheeks harden
to marble. when you try try try
to keep her safe from men
like you, knowing there will always be men
like you, i will be there.
someday, not now, i will be there
in her eyes, a ghost
you cannot wash off, a ghost
whose name rushes back like poison,
a quiet justice, near biblical.
you won't tell her about me then—
there's no need to speak of such secrets.
the weight you must carry thereafter
will be sunset enough.

HOME SAYS GO BACK TO WHERE YOU CAME FROM

as a child, i would not let my country hold me.
thought i was too jagged for her red arms,
thought she could never kiss my two toned edges.

on my eighteenth birthday, i run to a new home.
and home says *your blood scares us,*
thick contagious gold. your skin, your eyes,
and my god, how you walk,
chest full of pride
despite it all.

after years of unlearning my radiance,
i find myself in a small chinese restaurant
where i order shāo mài in my mother tongue.
the waiter wipes his dampened cheeks,
presses his hand to his heart and says *thank you.*
you sound like home. there, in upstate new york,
we cry in a language no one else can understand.

and i wonder if as a child, i told my country *i am not like you*
when i meant *i cannot love*
what looks like me, when i cannot bear
to look at me.

but she is my mother. even when i am split down
the middle, mind
from body, i wear her like the world.
even when i slammed the door on her fingers,
she unhinged herself from its wood to remind me
if it gets hard out there,

remember you always have a place to come back to.

on my twenty-second birthday, the world
turns to wreckage, and wreckage
turns to mirrors. my family nails their eyes to the tv,
cold black pacific. and when it lights up,
my face is attached to every innocent asian body
lying limp in the street. a garden of peonies
seeping rubies into stolen soil.

our blood, thick, contagious gold.
our skin, an endless scroll of silk.
our hands are a quiet expanse,
a cloud of fire. and it scares them,
my god, it scares them. how we walk,
chest full of pride
because of it all.

on my twenty-second birthday, home
says *go back to where you came from*
and i do. home
says *go back to where you came from*
and i think *what a privilege*
to know where i came from. what a privilege
that even if i silence the beijing peonies, the callouses
on my family's backs from carrying history, the smell
of mama's jiǎo zī, the waves of victoria harbor
singing me to sleep, marry a white man
and erase my name, marry a knife
and erase my face, still
i will pass on my goldskin to my daughters,
the warmth of a land
that refuses to abandon her children.

HEAVEN, BACKWARDS

in the end, not all stories get to be told.
uncle hands me auntie's old headscarf.
in america, they say things about me. things that aren't true. so
i am not home. there are times all my words sound like
maybe ma keeps the baby. maybe the war leaves after it is finished.
the gravestone under my hands is all the winters where
my body, too, failed to make them know
why auntie did not cry before the first surgery.
on my nineteenth birthday, a lump forms on my rib cage and i understand
my uncle never believed in heaven, but
when the chemo stopped working, he smiled and said *i will be with my sister soon.*
i always skip arts & crafts for the hospice.
later, i ask the nurse for the wifi password so auntie can learn to tie a headscarf.
it's okay to just listen, the teacher says.
the poems in me cannot speak english yet, but
i can tell a story and bring them all to life again. at least let me try.

continued...

i can tell a story and bring them all to life again. at least let me try.

the poems in me cannot speak english yet. *but*

it's okay to just listen, the teacher says.

later, i ask the nurse for the wifi password so auntie can learn to tie a headscarf.

i always skip arts & crafts for the hospice.

when the chemo stopped working, he smiled and said *i will be with my sister soon;*

my uncle never believed in heaven. but

on my nineteenth birthday, a lump forms on my rib cage and i understand

why auntie did not cry before the first surgery.

my body, too, failed to make them know.

the gravestone under my hands is all the winters where

maybe ma keeps the baby. maybe the war leaves after it is finished.

i am not home. there are times all my words sound like

in america, they say things about me. things that aren't true. so

uncle hands me auntie's old headscarf.

in the end, not all stories get to be told.

A PORTRAIT OF MEDUSA
or, in response to "why do you still write about milbank?"

some of it can be art. but not the sheets i threw out
because of the blood. and not the blood.

not the almost empty movie theatre, the broken wine bottle,
the black velvet dress. not the earrings on his dresser.

not the exoskeleton of what i hoped to be true about nineteen
draped over his closet door,

not piecing together poems with any word except
the word. *there are some things you're not allowed*

to write about. a doe will hang by its neck
on the eaves of milbank. they will leave her there all winter

to see what drains out. then, they will take her tongue
and bury it by the sycamore tree.

those that search for truth only from the mouths they can accept
are unconcerned with truth. so let this narrative continue.

there was no curse. i was born a monster.
i did not crawl out of his room cradling my teeth

in my mouth. it did not take three years to swallow them all.
they did not become seeds. the human body absorbs nothing.

in this story, which may be
the story, an animal hovers over a building

occupied only in memory. in this story,
a girl becomes a woman becomes a monster

even perseus won't dare approach.
another man will not undo me.

i will hold my own head to the gods like a lantern,
a torsoless sun with a thousand open eyes.

on that day, my tongue will bloom too.
but i won't return to it anymore.

there are some things i can only write about.

I GIVE MYSELF SEVEN DAYS TO LEAVE YOU

monday

      i return to the concrete building, a lexicon of sunlight.
      there, mornings slowly fill to the brim,
      adorned for a great engagement. even the night
      tastes of licorice and incense.
      it is may, and i am twenty, forever.

tuesday

      after the miscarriage, mama said *i knew the first one*
      wasn't gonna make it. seven months
      and i hardly slept. what's meant to be
      will never make you that miserable.

wednesday

      a dove dives into a window,
      her wings twitching, a final prayer for flight.

thursday

      when i say *i love myself* loudly,
      chest up, full of teeth,
      and ask about you in the same breath,
      my blood bleaches itself white with guilt.

friday

      memory works like an old brush,
      moving through the same patch of canvas
      until it conceals what it needs to. the voice
      is the first to go.

saturday

      i reread old poems like an archaeologist,
      studying buried bones as if they were newborn.
      i tell myself *this is okay.*
      at least i kept those stories somewhere.
      somewhere they can't hurt me anymore.

sunday

ODE TO THE CRAZY GIRL LABEL

shame is the first charm they look for in a woman,
yet your blood is tranquil in its intensity.
they've never seen rubies catch fire like that,

so of course they run. and of course they look back
when they do. the fear you induce is irresistible.

your ardent heart, your colored skin,
the instrument of your throat
birthing its song from a tongueless well—
when your existence is a marvel,
loving yourself is necromancy.

still, you persisted in this magic.
you nourished your body, once fluent in shattering,
as if it were both god and church.
you cut open the stomach of betrayal,
used its caverns as canvas. you told the truth.
it did not matter if they listened.

what else were you supposed to do,
let them wear philomela's tongue
as a fashion statement? step back
into the bathtub? grieve
your straight, male, perfect, dead sibling to life,
to become his shadow? be
sixteen again?

lilith was exiled from eden's grip
and became the queen of demons.

medusa was mutilated into a monster,
and with the same curse,
became a goddess.

they loved you more when you were sick,
but you no longer live to be loved.

so if *crazy* is the only sun
that illuminates your silhouette,
glow, regardless.

WHAT WE GAVE EACH OTHER

first, my living poems with breath and blood. each little moon,
another universe where history dances backwards, back
to the orange streetlights, to the spine of summer.

then, calloused hands, paint stains, bleached fingertips.
each curve of the wrist and twist of the blade,
a prayer: were i to lose you, i'd want to lose you
bearing the callouses of my ancestors' warzone heels.
i'd want to wave a white flag
sculpted from the bones in my knuckles,
left exposed after each mile i dug to you.
i'd want to lose you from one limb to the next.

you gave me a black sky, a widening gyre.
the mouth of language, never large enough
to fit the tongues of regret.
i sit on the red couch for two or three seasons,
the womb of darkness cooking my light
until she glows like the tuscan sun.

you left to mother this bulging, living thing.
at dawn, she nibbles holes in my belly,
trying to get out. at dusk,
she thirsts for your blood, cool clean milk.
i feel her poems that no longer have an audience
to bleed for—*these will have to do.*

one day, the loneliness will exit,
holy and new, wearing my face.
i am growing the courage to accept this gift.

ANNIVERSARY POEM

bury the silent flight to moscow,
unspoil the meat in the kitchen.

wipe off the mud, unearth the dead,
unspill the wine from the carpet.

break every clock that reminds us of summer,
sing of the home we do not remember,
release your name from my mother's ears.

unlearn the lessons, unknow the wound,
let me conceive this power elsewhere.

only then can we return to the tennis court
perfumed with blackberries and musk,

when poetry needn't swell to poems,
and the will to forgive was forgiveness enough.

IN OTHER WORDS,

1. auntie used to tell stories about the man in the hospice
who called her by his wife's name.
every morning he'd look into the small square window, a frame
for the canvas of his halo. by noon he'd give her
his chocolate pudding and sticky rice. at night he'd ask
if the room was warm enough. said she always
liked the house warmer, even in summers.
for three months, auntie held his speckled hands and said
the nurses told me she left thirty years ago
and took everything with her. the bed, the desk,
the music player. the whole house was empty when you came here,
until she started answering.

2. the day i left new york, i walked to the third floor of milbank
and touched the door where i entered as *girl* and left as *ghost.*
the henna of my shadow is still there. trying to find a body.

3. once, i ate love like a serpent's tail. i'd rather it be this way
than to be nineteen for three more years. a doe in the glen.
branches threading in and out like string,
bleeding poetry in chunks on the moss.

4. the home that raised me lies stillborn in lilac mist.
we buried something in the land, and return to it
only in the space between reliving and forgetting.
this, beyond anything, is true:
no one can go home after they've left.

5. growing up, all my mother knew was hunger and snow.
her tiny fingers would turn violet at night.

all the kids on the border drank vodka to stop from freezing to death.
their bellies, an auditorium. their throats, an endless belt of bone.
until one day grandpa took his dog and hung him
on the biggest tree in the forest, dragged his body back
and made soup for the whole village.
he shook with each cut. *i loved him too. but if you're gonna let love*
kill you like that, then you're a fool.

6. once, two people dreamt the same dream
long before they met. they knew,
and did not care.

7. on his deathbed the man called for auntie one last time.
he traced the indents on her arms where the scars were.
the warmth of her palms, his perfect hallucination.
i'm sorry. thank you. i just wanted her back.

8. purgatory is a bisected manhattan
sinking into the earth along 45th street.
she looks into the bruised landscape,
half moons bitten into the skyline, a frame
for the canvas of her halo. and says *let's jump.*
the first few seconds of falling
feel like flying. he agrees.
and together, they hold hands on the edge of a cliff
until they turn to stone.

THE DREAM WHERE I SEE THE BEGINNING OF IT ALL

spraying perfume in the bathroom
to cover up the smell of antiseptic. pressing buttons
on the broken vending machine. in the house
we had to sell. auntie, uncle, grandma, grandpa
lie baby blue on beds that look like curved boats
heading somewhere they can never
tell me about. in this dream my hands are small.
tiny globes that have yet to learn
what they're capable of. that to be a poet
means to forgive your inability to forget. mom and dad melt
into the ground. grandma looks at me
with my eyes. she reminds me *art was worthless during the war*
and it sounds like *what's the use of love*
if it is not a cure. in this dream
i see the beginning of it all; i write
four letters to god. tuck them under my bed. before
i move to new york, i carve each one into a different urn
in the order the ocean takes them. even now,
i remember the glow of their steel blue fingertips
beneath my guilty heat. even now,
my clean body says *i love you, you, you, you,*
and the words only make ripples on the surface.
my clean body says *bleed into me. let me carry*
what's inside your bones. and your bones
are buried too deep underwater to hear me.

CICADAS

a poem for upstate new york

my left eye sits in the gap
between the concrete wall and the twin bed
with knife marks on the side.
my legs, placed on the iris of a frozen lake.
my virgin skin, taken
by some winter that lasted all year.
i pass by a meat market in beijing and see,
in the window, a girl
walking out of the forest with no legs.
she falls in front of a priest and cries *hell is real.*
hell is real. hell is what we do to each other.
heaven is to forget what has been done.
to say i hated you, more than most,
would be an understatement. to claim
i wouldn't pluck out my voice, too,
just to hate you again
would be a lie. isn't this what home means?
to recognize what no longer recognizes you.
to return, in dreams, woven between the trees,
where cicadas first sang in sync to your secrets.
to return, a stranger
bloodlinked to the land.

RECOUNT OF LAST NIGHT'S DREAM

suddenly i'm thirty, living with a partner in the city i love,
still dreaming of you at the age we were when they found you.
a tall, fragile sparrow, neck cracked purple,
wings dangling like electric cords.

suddenly i'm thirty and you are both the boy in bryant park
with ice cream drips on his dinosaur hoodie
and the white-haired man in a leather wheelchair.
you may even be the soccer player at the bodega buying a pack of menthols.

suddenly it's been september for eleven years
and i am standing outside our home, our home
built entirely from the weight of *too late,*
watching the light in your room flicker on and
off and on and off and on
until it goes out for the last time.

even when dreaming i say nothing.
even when dreaming i do not save you.

instead, i stand outside
carving these useless poems into the crooked tree.
these poems that sound nothing like your grandchildren's voices,
look nothing like your laugh lines.
waiting for the light to turn on.

WHAT THE LIVING MUST DO

i imagine the green tinted couch,
its bruised insides left to sour
for three more years, the clothes
hung lopsided in your closet,
still creased, as if to remember
touch, i imagine the books
splayed open on your desk, uncertain
of their continuance, and most of all,
i imagine the bowl of fruit
by your bedside, half eaten
when the police came in. i imagine
holding that bowl, an orange
split down the middle, an apple
already rotting, a few grapes
torn from the stem, their juices
clinging to my skin, trying
to convince me they have seeped out
from my own hands,
and i imagine myself standing there,
destroyed by the absolute need
to wash it off.

THE NIGHT YOU DIED I DREAMT OF A HUMMINGBIRD OUTSIDE MY WINDOW

for j.

i could barely hear it sing,
but i saw its wings
beating against the wind, as if
they had known flight
beyond this lifetime.
i pressed my hands to the glass
and imagined you, too, were somewhere
in the sky, wings stretched out
in open air, still trying to sing.

DOUBLE HELIX

i have long forgotten the cursive of your breath,
if it feels anything like growing up
in summers that lasted all year. they say
that's not how it works. summer is
dead. yet we spit out our milk teeth
and knot into each other again, a narrative
braided from dead land. do you remember
the orange streetlights framing the edges
of our old courtyard? they've followed me
well into adulthood. i think i'll always
love like that. like two rows of warm light
spilling onto the sidewalk, the chapel, the soft earth,
until nothing remembers the cold. isn't this
the home we've missed? sitting here,
coated in blood orange, fearlessly tethered
to what we cannot touch. even
dirty, even dead, i wanted to be the moss
trailing up those red brick walls. leave my blood there,
there, there, freckling the sky, leaking
onto easton's moonstone shoulders. how curious
that this time, summer has become every season
and none. a serpent eating its own tail, an emerald sun
watching history dance backwards
until we return to the same beginning. how curious
that our collisions are only to remember love
with a mouth full of milk teeth. a light
that wakes our dead home, makes her sit up and smile,
knowing her magic is not done yet.

GOODBYE TO ALL THAT

eight thousand miles away, your home begins
to loosen your memory into the clouds.
you say *i'm coming back. wait for me. i am not done
yet.* and the ocean buries your promises.
an open mouth of saltwater and longing.
nothing travels that far and stays
intact.

she, whose mind was carved from the same clay as yours,
moves to san francisco. and your grief coils into itself,
knowing you were the one to leave first.

he, who you could not say goodbye to
because what else would you remember childhood by,
buys a new place in seattle
and you pretend to forget each other for eight more years.

she, who made your summers burst into stardust,
sends a text after seven months in melbourne:
new york is nothing like how we left it.

the mildew scent of weekends in suburbia,
the red couch in the dimly lit cafe.
the broken jukebox, the late drives to nowhere,
the curving avenue that smelled of violets and trashwater,
the laughably inauthentic chinese food you never complained about
because you didn't need that to belong anymore—

forever is a series of nows.
but there's no warning when your present
consists entirely of recollection.

FAME

a butterfly soaring through the sky
dreaming of her cocoon

MOONGLOW

he called your eyes champagne diamonds.
said he wanted the world behind them so bad
he had to cut them out of your skull
and wear them as jewelry. his presence,
so ghostly it moved like peace,
taught you to lie on his chest and whisper *my eyes shine brighter*
around your neck. his closeness, a simple hallucination,
made the raven in you tear its wings off
and become human; the sky
couldn't hold you like he did.

what did you expect? your big love is full,
always. she pierces continents to retrieve her diamonds,
tossed away like old stones. she nurses the carcass of her softness
back to health, only to be washed ashore,
time after time, more shattered than the last.

you thought he couldn't smell the salt on you?
you're drowning in your giving.
he knows he can drink your heartblood until he's moonglowing,
and you will never wilt. look at the excess
pooling on his bedroom floor. another slice of seascape
drifting him away from you. how do you force the ocean
to take the shape of a man?

you cannot make someone unlearn
overloving them as permission
to underlove you.

and so you are abandoned.
your clear crystal aura, your boundless expanse.
a final confirmation that those who do not deserve to keep you,
never will.

I'LL NEVER TAKE THE EXIT OFF HIGHWAY 78

once, there were celestine sheets and nectarines.
the indent in your mint green wallpaper,
a dimple in june.

in time, everything returns to the earth.
but i thought what was claimed so violently,
protected so fiercely, loved that much,
could never die.

like a rose to its hue, i am bound to you.
your tigereye sun, your starlit body.
the bow of your spine, the curve of your mouth.
a part of me still laced into your marrow.

now home is a dead dog i wait by the door to feed.
home is a dress hanging stillborn in my closet,
haunted by its memory of flesh.

at night, the last of your light unhooks from my eyes
and tries to travel towards the yellowwood tree.
i catch it in my hands and say *we can't*
go home. we can never
go home. despite what we promised each other
in those infinite summers,
we must try to find that feeling
elsewhere.

COLLISION

today my universe passed by like a stranger
afraid to make eye contact,
and i felt my hands swell with the chartreuse of your july,
the halo of your june, longing for a page to spill for.

once, you had the color of spring
and the ecstasy of summer.
once, you made me real. real
enough to know that a wanting,
so deep it mirrors frenzy,
is still not fatal.
real enough to know that love can happen twice,
without losing its meaning.

so put our stories back to sleep.
it will never be, but must be enough
that our mere collision, against all odds,
was a miracle.

SUMMER EIGHT THOUSAND MILES AWAY FROM YOU

you liked the way i raised hell with each syllable.
ruined, reckless splashes of red on canvas
oblivious to color.

you liked the way i was the first name
that took your whole body to pronounce,
that i reminded you of dizzying, terrifying
freedom. a brand new convertible
and a tank full of gas.
that you could compare me to anything but rosewater.

still, we dug out each other's rot with teeth
till we bled blackberry blood—the ink
i mistook as understanding.

i tell you my aunt died drowning in kindness yet retained a flame beneath her face.
i tell you within my scars are the endings to stories she never finished writing.
i tell you that is why i will never finish writing.
you tell me about the boy who can't walk anymore,
knowing your tendency to press your soul to someone else's mouth
just to whisper *i don't want you.*

i raise hell with each syllable,
i take whole cities to pronounce,
i am terrifying
freedom, i am every woman
who came before me.

god bless the months that pulled me away from you,
the miles that stood between us like a third body.

god bless my mother's attitude festering in my stomach,
my grandma's tongue sitting pretty in my throat,
swearing in verse at every move unmade.
god bless my hands for snapping me back from this pitless sky
because of no grandiose betrayal, no public revenge,
other than the realization that generations of women
have burned down the houses they built
for men who never wanted homes,
to train themselves in the desperate act
of unloving the unavailable.

OUR STORY, TOLD IN THE WRONG ORDER

11. i kiss the stump of my ring finger
to clean our *what ifs* out of my skin.

2. christmas lights flutter alive in shinjuku,
my phone screen follows its glow. this black frame,
a glass wall where i cannot touch you, only watch
as our breath turns to raindrops on the surface.
i open my notes app and begin writing.
the source of this feeling, a sea of marigolds.
connection owes a certain reliance to history.
eight years later, this poem still only has one line:
december was the warmest month.

6. summers in new york smell like apricots and rain.
i pull out the right love from the back of my throat,
a ballerina spinning in my music box mouth,
and misplace it.
spend the next six months piecing together
the shards of her porcelain.

9. i delete and re-add your number every day for three weeks.

8. i write twelve verses to no one.
by noon they all sound the same:
you only wanted me as a ghost.

7. six months later, i send: *happy birthday. hope you're doing good.*
and we return in a perfect hallucination, a reminder of bodies.
we pour into each other as if we were made of water,
yet continue to cover up each excuse

like dressing an open wound.

4. your returning comes, always, in a mosaic of pixels.
i drive upstate from a budding manhattan,
thinking *what magic that this darkened expanse*
lights up to halos
to bring you back to me.

12. i brush by the same cities we promised each other,
peer into each cavern of sunset until i find the right shade of future.
someone said there's an angel hidden in the gardens,
mama says there's always blood in the riverbanks.
one day i will read my poems in seattle and not think of you.
one day i will find proof that anything disguising itself
as endurance is not love.

3. we do not talk for one year.

5. we do not talk for two years.

1. legs crossed, hair pulled into a high ponytail.
i brush a layer of black paint over my bike
and tuck my phone between two ninth grade textbooks.
we've been talking for about a week now.
you make me smile. i tell no one.

10. i cut my ring finger off with mama's kitchen knife
and purge the words i've swallowed for eight years.
"For stony limits cannot hold love out,
And what love can do, that dares love attempt"
a pilgrimage never begun, a body heavy with oceans,
a slow fall that never leaves the ground.

slide to answer

THE LOVERS

IF I NEVER STOP TURNING YOU TO POETRY

my dog died during the pandemic
while i was quarantined in another country

her legs had been paralyzed for years but on the last night
she dragged her limp body to the front porch
picked up a pair of my old slippers
and carried them into the doghouse with her

that's how she died

alone, hurting, holding on to the scent of home
that could never come home to her

THE PERFECT TRINITY

his voice tightens like a firm grip, her bones become a chamber
shifting to his command. an angular window
opened just enough to smell the ocean.
roasted dates, a plate of sliced papayas.
the oculus of a spotless dinner table glistening with pride.
didn't we teach you not to talk back?

he is the hand. she is the gun. and you
are dreaming of what it would feel like
to be a girl with a bracelet of a voice.
to be created as anything other than a bullet
swelling with the heat of her shatter,
waiting to pierce the body of the world.

CLINTON, FROM HERE

your scent appears in ribbons, invading
my space like the shape of a stranger
i could have known.

the waves of victoria harbor,
its hysteric crashing, its hopeless rhythm,
contort into a chorus of footsteps
aching to trace the streets that hurt me into myself.

yet i stay, for family, future, correctness,
safety. stagnant,
here, bearing the saltwater like moonstones in my stomach,
jealous of how my life lives on without me.

HOME COUNTRY

i ask my first home not to kill me.
so she hands over a roof of iron nails, a bed of needles
threading in and out of my abdomen. years later,
i am still trying to digest her love language.

split my blood between the seawater of victoria harbor
and the streets of saint petersburg. let beijing separate
bone from muscle, cartilage from tissue.
give one eye to pennsylvania, the other to clinton.
leave my lungs for east village.

my second home is dirty. she smells of jasmine and regret,
chantilly and cigarette smoke. she struts down spiral staircases
with fake designer shoes and mismatched socks.
she's raw, rude, and unafraid.
she is the electricity of one night
and the lifetime of remembering that follows.
she is the home that does not want me.

my third home and i remain on nodding terms.
she allows me to wear my scars like white lace,
but they are still scars. i am still history.

if you go back far enough, i am both
the girl leaving her burning village behind
and the soldier she is running from.
which is to say, no one can teach my body
to stop fighting for
and against itself.

every time i make art in a language
that pushes my mother tongue deeper into my skull,
every time i sleep soundly in a city
that cannot pronounce my birth name,
the earth beats me black and blue
until these bruises begin to paint the flag
of a country that does not yet exist.

COLLAR

out the window a girl
kind smile hair down
to her waist walking
her rottweiler
fur black as coal she
drags her by a leash imported
from another country i see her
every day on empty streets by
familiar buildings from
my bedroom window she
never looks up changes
pace keeps
moving i see her
every day the way her smile
bleeds the dog
has a home
an address a street name
a number engraved
on her collar the girl
no one knows for sure

EASTON

next time i walk down the streets
we used to call home
i'll make sure
to unzip
my old winter coat
down to the chest

to let
the ghosts
back in

IN WHICH I REWRITE POEMS ABOUT YOU TO BE ABOUT ANYTHING ELSE

ghosts and poetry are the twins of neglect,
constantly finding each other for the first time.
one, a tongue. the other, a voice.

here: a bluebird the size of a jewelry box
circles your city, and when you do not see her,
writes her own head into a wall without complaint.

here, a house is introduced to erase the bodies in the ground.

TAXIDERMY

My life is a flight and I lose everything and everything belongs to
oblivion, or to him. I do not know which of us has written this page.

—Jorge Luis Borges, *Borges and I*

let me begin
do other animals who feel
so precisely that pieces
pour into something
tangible know
before the chemicals enter whether
they are begging the gods
to preserve the illusion
of life or life
itself there is a girl
on the wall and she is not
the one asking these
questions let me begin
again i am a cascade and you
are the shape that holds water
i will endlessly pour
into you let me begin
again i was born to endlessly pour
into you let me
begin when i was six i told
my best friend when i die
i want my ashes mixed into paint
packaged in tiny silver tubes and sold
in the art store on lexington let me
begin i wonder if the illusion of life
and life itself are any different
if no one can tell

again i look towards the girl
on the wall and no one can tell
the difference i let her hair
fall on my shoulders i let her
walk down lexington wearing my face
my death will trigger the delivery
of her let me
begin there is no other way
to cheat mortality
than to be consumed

WAITING

the waiting sprouts in the purgatory of my stomach.
she grows glasseyes, cherry lips, baby bones.
i tell her *when the time is right*
as she drinks up my organs. my pink fluid,
her holy eucharist.

i beg the sky for tragedy. give me the arguments in the kitchen,
crying in your sister's car, running out in october rain
just to come home and fall asleep next to each other
in the bedroom with the beige wallpaper, spines kissing.
let me churn oceans, let me scrape my knees to ribbons
with every mile i crawl to you.

or carry me, the hollowed cavern of my body, my body
withered and bulging, a belly of veins.
and hang me, leg first, on the bed.
do not listen when i say *i have mothered the waiting*
for eight years. i would have held her
for eight hundred more.

choke my baby out with the moirai's gold thread.
watch her blood splash across the stone floor.
a rosy bud cut from its stem
one day before spring comes.

THE ONLY STORY I KNOW.

in this story, persephone does not sink into hell
nor stay above ground. instead,
she lingers in the in-between space.

the poems unmuzzle themselves and speak in metallic tones.
blend into this saccharine ache. even if he said
what you wanted him to, the love
would never have been as golden as the pain.

in this story, persephone does not sink into hell
and instead,
lingers.

we fight. you ignore me for three days
and i write another angry poem.
we pretend to leave each other for the theatrics,
then return to the room overlooking the park.
you joke about my sunglasses.
i say none of what the poems say.

in this story, which did not have to be
the only story,
you open my mask and find a heart.
i open your heart to find a mask.

persephone does not sink into hell
nor stay above ground. instead,
she lingers in the in-between space.

in this story, i say *i would have burned for you.*
you say none of what your heart says.
so i continue writing this story,

A BROKEN DOUBLE SONNET ON YOUR NEW GIRL

she will be the kind of girl i've always dreamed i could be.
her translucent skin, so clear you can trace the lavender of vein.
her thin thighs, her flat stomach, her curled lashes.
her kiss will be peach honey tea. your sister will call her *pretty*.
your mother will call her *stable*. she will not have pieces of bone
stuck between another man's teeth, her eyes lost across continents,
her life before eighteen sealed as an untold story.
she will tell you *you're doing your best* even when you are not.
she will never push you. she will never question. she will not be me,
with this harshness that only grows from softness left out to rot.
with these words scraping against the blade of your cowardice.
she will know trust as an instinct instead of a luxury.
she will not be full of contradictions. kind and ruthless.
insane and rational. beautiful and hell.

your new girl will be a gentle voice,
asking *what do you want for dinner?* instead of
let's live in seven countries this year. just pack up and go.
and when you leave her,
her pain will be a smokeless fire.
not so blinding, so public.
you will leave and stay gone this time,
without these poems that exaggerate what really happened
into what could have happened. what might've happened. what did
happen. without these poems telling you without
telling you *the most tragic part is how we stopped trying.*
her body will not be more scar than skin.
she will not feel guilty for the way she opens.
she will not be me. she will not be me.

BEFORE THE FUTURE COMES

i'll linger above my city,
lodged in midair,
preparing for the soar
of a bird, the shatter
of a bullet.

THE STARVING DOG

or, in which an anonymous user comments "good riddance" to the international student trying to return home during a global pandemic

watching him
lick his bowl clean
as i bite my tail off
for food.
believing him
when he tells me
this is my home
too.

TO BE ASIAN, NOW
written during the coronavirus pandemic

how godly, to be asian,
now, and love yourself.
a covenant of history, a scripture
to our goldblood. to be asian,
now, is to be the sun
shining, also, shining,
still, on those who both consume
and condemn its light.
when the world is a torch, to be asian,
now, is to be a witch
refusing to burn.

DREAMING OF BLUEBELLS

when he leaves, the delirium of closeness,
near lilylike, will sway around the room
to prepare for its asphyxiation.

you asked for this. yet every time, you wonder
why you're never more than a story
laced with threads of surrealism.

turn to the mirror. the silver lakes echoing ripples
in your image. if you could just sit for a while,
beneath the bluebells,
and be silent. if you could just
hold conversations about wallpaper,
make him boiled eggs for breakfast,
and be silent.

but even the bluebells make you dream of oceans
kneeling at your feet.

stone woman, daughter of lilith.
fearless, horrifying, intolerably unashamed.
your scarlet heels click to the rhythm of blossoming rage.
your hair is the same shade as the filth that makes a city look alive.
the flick of your liner reminds him of a frontflip stage dive,
the distorted bass pounding through a crowd.

look at yourself. your mouth kindles
an amnesiac trance, your hips are smooth thunderstorms.
you bite down on the world, and the world
wears your mark around its neckline.

you are the kind of woman they tell stories about,
yet won't return for.

and how does that feel?
to be so transient, so immortal.
both masculine and goddess,
feminine and king.

if he wants to leave, hold the door open.
tuck your love inside yourself, put it to sleep with a gentle needle,
next to the pinkwater, next to your mother tongue,
next to childhood.

you are a fantasy
the weak don't have the guts
to sink their teeth into.

VAN GOGH'S SEVERED EAR AND AN ARTIST'S PROCESS OF HEALING

nobody does that unless they're truly mad.
every night i slit open memory like the belly of a plum
and watch as the juices lay handprints around the room.

he didn't just remove a section, he cut the entire damn thing off.
place my love in a silver box,
wrap it in silk, gift it to some poor boy in kirkland
whose screams dance through the woods.

one slice, one razor, and it was done.
i am tired of carving out new poems for the same men
with different names.

he spent the whole night trying to stop the bleeding.
what else is there to being an artist?
to turn grief into food and feed the dead
until color returns to their cheeks.
to nurse your wounds until they rearrange into a new limb
and watch as a knife appears in your hand.

AFTER THE BREAKUP

a bird will fly into my bedroom window
the long angular one lurking
above new york city
the one that would fog up
between november and december
glow cidergold in the summer
when i go out the bird
will be still breathing still
alive
lying in her own blood
limbs outstretched as if reaching
across half empty sheets i'll think
what a waste of something so beautiful
and dream about stitching her wounds with silver string
feeding her little worms and attention
giving her my chest as a bed to rest in
my arms as a safe place to heal
before your voice swims in from behind my skull
easier to just let it die

THE MUSIC BOX

in first grade my mother sent me to ballet school
to become a woman. i remember lacing up my white silk shoes,
training my stumpy legs to move as feathers,
and most of all, the spinning ballerina locked
inside the music box on my dresser.

after two years of dancing they pulled my mother aside.
said *your daughter is not the kind of girl we're looking for.*
she moves like something is on fire.
her legs send currents into the earth.
she's too much, everywhere.

i went home that day, took a hammer from my father's toolshed,
smashed the music box to pieces, and swore
to forget. forget her ballerina legs, her porcelain skin,
forget pinching my stomach in the changing room,
forget the shards exposed on the floor.

imagine my utter lack of surprise when you said i intrigued you
because i was the *craziest woman you'd met.*

see, old habits die a slow death.
it takes a lifetime to forget and one instant to return, return
to the comfort of a mouth that both shelters
and smothers.

for a while, you were the line
and i was the kite soaring across a collapsing sky.
your normalcy, a quiet narcotic.
yet your attempt to tame me was the fiercest fire you've sparked.

even my sweetness reeks of insanity,
even my grace clings to thunder,
a certain, strange delicacy in how much space they demand.

i am not the pleasant body trapped inside your music box mouth.
i am the way the hammer felt against the heat of my palms.

CANDY LIQUOR

how afraid were you of the tongue
that braids into the gut? forgiveness
is candy liquor. it sinks to my stomach,
burns the whole way down. mama said to love
is to open yourself up to slaughter. i have done my part already,
and learned that none of this is romantic. this pilgrimage of ash.
this martyrdom. these questions i do not ask
because i no longer expect you
someday, when you're ready, when it's easy,
to look your desire in the face. we sleep scarless
in different cities yet have the audacity to claim
we tried everything. how curious
that retreat is almost pressing your lips to your dream.
only close enough to feel the exchange of air. how curious
that a warm house is still not a home
if you refuse to turn the key.

EXTRACT THIS SOFT FEELING

now, my hands are those of surgeons.
they have trained themselves to replace my eyes,
the ones burned to opals, every time, with new ones.
just so i can continue staring into the sun a bit longer.

you say, of course, that you never learned how to love.
i mop away my boot prints trailing down the tail of minos
from when i begged him to retrieve my residue where another man left it,
just to have something pure to give you. but perhaps there's nothing
to grieve here.

with my hands i flay eden's flowers.
with my tears i exorcize the photographs that did not gray fast enough.
with my bones i deny the ghostchild in pennsylvania,
still dancing with you in that borrowed space.

i call to the wind, i call to the darkblood—
come bat-winged and lucid.
the way she first held me in her womb.

extract this soft feeling fuming from chest to hip,
lay it out on the operating table so i can talk to it like a dead sibling
when i know for certain it cannot hurt me back.

some demons have the voices of ex lovers
each accompanied by futures forged in fever dreams.
my demons sound like every second i wasted offering a full heart to half a man.

let others walk the ceremonious walk.
leave me unafflicted.

without you i think with two heads.
with you i think with none.

MAYBE TOMORROW

i will turn over every city we almost moved to,
look under every bed i've slept in without you,
behind the red couch in the college cafe
when i promised to leave this town for good,
around the mudstained swing set
still creaking against the smallest gust of wind,
by the streetlights in pennsylvania
collecting dust since we turned sixteen,
between each poem, each word, each letter i wrote
when you were my summer in new york snow,

and find the absence of grief
instead of the absence of you.

THE INABILITY TO EXPRESS ONESELF DUE TO THE INADEQUACY OF LANGUAGE

> Unhappy that I am, I cannot heave
> my heart into my mouth.
>
> —William Shakespeare, *King Lear*

what i mean is i have returned everything
i took to saint petersburg to its rightful place
except the longing. what i mean is in another town
that grew the same houses as this one, a baby sparrow
learns to fly after six broken bones. what i mean is we run
from each other in different ways. what i mean is we drift
towards each other in the same way. what i mean is
nana said i got a pen when she got a gun. nana said
stay young even when you're old. nana said *be happy. at least
try. or i would've survived the war for nothing.* what i mean is
i have loved with my heart once, then with my mind.
now i must love with my gut.

if poetry is performance, crown me lear.
if poetry is an eternal stone in the chest, a sisyphean love
language will always try and fail to seize, hang me
with the bloodstring this mutilated machine weaves.
"What shall Cordelia speak? Love, and be silent."

THE FRIEND

it is impossible to remember you
without remembering god
living in the collection of your knuckles.

what makes this so unholy?
the maroon couch, the peach carpet, the night
straining rain-touched wind into the room,

and you, in a deep blue dress
hanging just below the knees.

even buried, even silent, this story reminds me
the truest gift asks for nothing in return.

except, perhaps, a wish
that i am allowed

to keep searching for a place
where no country or institution can stop me
from wanting to be the warm glow of your fireplace

spreading light from the inside out.
unlike any prayer, gentle

& guiltless.

SUITCASES FROM COLLEGE

home is my jawbone broken clean off.
but i cannot grieve that.
so i'll grieve the winter coat.

the smell of the forest sunken into its leather.
i'll grieve the maroon bralette, the lighter
in the left pocket of the orange rainjacket—

i'll grieve only what can be returned to me.
three suitcases of old clothes,
a handful of teeth.

BURY IT

my honey hands tucked
into the jacket daddy bought
for the first day of
ninth grade the garden
draped itself in thick
snow he was much taller and much
older spun me
around a few times never
asked just
tried and tried and
did and i
drifted into the
sky that was the
ceiling five years
later in a room
the room that pinned me to another man's
ceiling i wonder if the garden
is what pinned me to his
ceiling why i played
dead pinned
to his ceiling hoping
it would fill the space
between his desire to take
and my desire to take
my tongue out
and bury it in the snow

TODAY I WATCHED A MOTH

fly into a fire and
out and
in and
in again with her
crisp little wings
and felt
relieved
that i am not the only one
who chose
to live like that

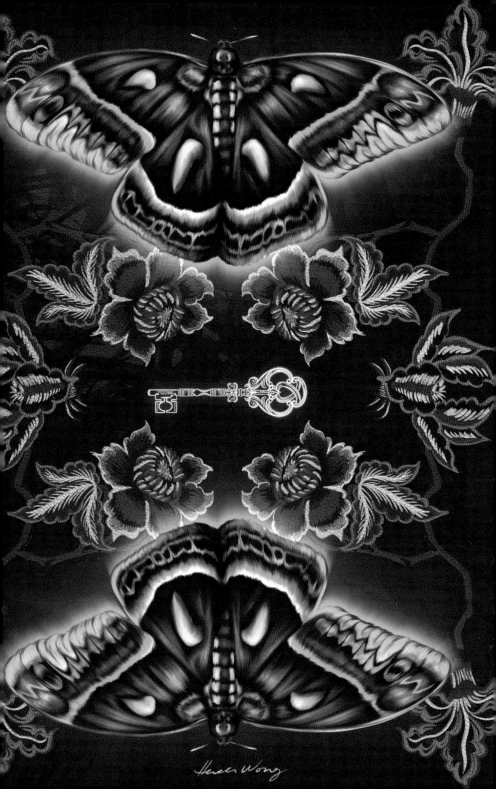

SAND

on the beach behind a house
that no longer exists, i
scoop up a handful of sand,
small beige pearls
beneath an hourglass
sky. and every time,
the tighter i try
to hold it, the faster
it leaks out of my hands.

AN ATHEIST COMES OUT TO GOD & NO ONE ELSE

pretend you did not know eve was made in lilith's image
after she was corrupted by man.

i bathe in what is left of my roots. they are holy,
they are exile, they are the way i dance

with my head pointed towards the moon.
so was it the bloodstained mattress

from sophomore year? was it the culture,
the country, the men with songbird voices

and switchblade hands? somewhere, there is a sliver
of a fifteen year old in a town that no longer exists,

watching another girl read *macbeth*
like she was the poetry. her cheekbones

gather july, her hair is the rust of a city
that glows of a kind adulthood.

but do not believe the words i say. in saying them,
i have already avoided the fate of a bird

who dies before she tastes flight.
so god, take my sky again. we both understand

why i cannot keep it. how long have you stayed silent
in the fear of becoming real?

WHEN HE MOVES TO MANHATTAN

tear the poster off the wall and take a piece
of the wall with it. there is not enough evidence here.
after a while, even the ghosts won't remember how they haunt.

i can already picture the skid marks from your mother's car
scarring the ground that once, too, clung to its purity.

your forgetting is easy—
folding that night into your suitcase and driving.
mine holds its own gravity.

when you move to manhattan, our home here
will gape open into a scream.
all this empty, all this hollow,
without a deserving body to project onto.

i will hook the hurt by its lips and feed it to the page.
i want my words to force you back into this room,
because i am not finished with you yet.

i will wear poetry as both perfume and armor.
rename *night*
as anything but your hands,

and notice, despite all that tries to rid my world of color,
the art is still here
and i am still here
to become it.

i will walk into a new room, choose
a shade of wallpaper reminiscent of,
yet entirely different from, the green we used to love.

when you leave,
i will build a home from the skeleton of the last,
and i will no longer think of you.

ODE TO ALL THE HAIR I'VE LOST SINCE JANUARY

the spider's eyes flicker like ghost diamonds.
he watches the new fly lie down, choose
to stay. i watch them
through the windows of my apartment
in a foreign city, the way he opens her
as if her whole body is an altar,

and peel off another chunk of hair.
silk still stuck to its roots,
a double helix of morn and night.
and remember when i, too,
did not seem to mind.

THE ANGEL WANTED TO FLY

i'll sell you my wings. i want a pair of arms.
the butcher grabs his meat cleaver,
the surgeon finds his needle. she was done
with those wings, those heavy
undead things. a secret
godless dialect. wilting magnolias
she could never get to speak. blood
cost or not, the angel wanted arms
to throw stones at the birds outside her window.
they must die they must die they must die.
to prove what she wants is impossible.

FOR HENRY

王 ; wong /wáng/
noun
1. king; monarch; prince

I know I have the body but of a weak and feeble woman;
but I have the heart and stomach of a king.
—Queen Elizabeth I, Speech to the Troops at Tilbury, 1588

Two hares running side by side close to the ground,
How can they tell if I am he or she?
—Unknown Author, "Ballad of Mulan," AD 386–535

let me tell this story from the beginning.
i grip the yellow marker with my whole hand.
every face, another sun. daddy leans over
to tell me a story. *midnight, the empty street,*
the house wasn't ours to begin with.
we had nowhere to go.

let me tell it from the beginning.
mama says *the miscarriage was hard. but his life*
would have been harder. daddy says
my daughter, one day
you will be the man of the house.

let me tell it. i've dreamt of your broad shoulders,
the ocean of your chest, full of a king's courage.
i grew up treading the tightrope
between too much and not enough
like the son you could never be.
close your legs, cut off those manic fingers.
no man could ever love a girl with a mouth like that.

did you leave your blood in mama's womb for me to eat up?
even one drop counts. maybe, then, your blood
turned into my eyes. my almond shaped rubies
housing the glare that makes men quiver.
or maybe it exploded into a heart. big enough
to eclipse mine, strong enough
to drain downwards. thick magnetic ink
hunting the wound of poetry.
or the top of my hairline, a ring of darkwater
that dares to lift continents.

let me tell this story.
my twin flame, my second shadow.
i eclipsed you, first.
my body is the ground you are buried in,
but i can memorialize you
without making a grave of my bones.

it is love that pushes me to crawl out from beneath you,
drenched in silky fluid. it is love that inscribes this oath:

i will claim the world so fiercely
that even the ghosts i carry
bow to my command.

this is the story i will tell my daughters.
i will tower over them, drip my warmth
onto their golden heads, hug them so tight
they almost blend into me again.

let me begin.
history writes not of a son who bears the name *king,*
but a daughter who learns to lift her lineage like a ghostcrown.

"At dawn she takes leave of the Yellow River,
In the evening she arrives at Black Mountain."

history demanded this emperor.
womanbodied, with a king's core.

ALTERNATE UNIVERSE IN WHICH I NEVER FOUND POETRY

my aborted brother turns in my mother's womb again.
i hold a cup of lóng jǐng with both hands,
waiting for him to come home
and reclaim the face stretched over my skull.

the dirt beneath the coffin lifts and a garden is unveiled.
my uncle and cousin step back into their car
and disappear for another decade.
the strangers peeling clementines at the funeral
go home to their daughters.
the iv bag overflows, the pills reappear,
auntie walks out of the earth as if it were a door.

my friend cuts himself down from his dorm room ceiling,
straightens his neck and walks into the dining hall.

i start eating healthier in case my dead aunt
needs a bone marrow transplant.

when another woman says she carries the weight
of what happens to us all, i will not tell her
that i, too, have fantasized about the first time
he holds his daughter. *there's no need to speak
of such secrets.*

something in me, something that began
the day i knew of language, continues
to fill the room with smoke.
but never speaks to me.

TURNING TO WALLPAPER

how do you hold the moon in your arms?
how do you drink her light?
my love goes for the jugular.
you push me away. i am blinding you.
i say *of course i'll wait. whenever you're ready.*
and forget, in the moment,
i am lying.

somewhere, it is mid-december and i am melting
behind the howling schoolyard, i am waking
to the burning church on broadway. i am,
every time a man looks at me, nineteen,
losing my eyes to his ceiling, leaving my tongue
on his ochre dresser, my legs on his nightstand.

so maybe this is what they mean by *survivor.*
apply heat to the caged rat and it will burrow itself into flesh
until it tastes the open air.
a bug dives headfirst into the web, loses one limb,
and lives.

loud woman. not sorry. not dying
to be claimed. i walk into a room
and become the room. he says *i'll love you
when you become the wallpaper.*

maybe this is a journey that consists of returning,
but returning to yourself demands a price.
the cage expands into a house, but you are still
drowning. so slice your human neck
for a pair of gills. this, too, is poetry.

to choose grief over love when the staying shrinks you.
to take your own hand and vow
to never again imagine yourself in the arms of those
who would have loved you if you were softer, smaller,
less whole, less alive.
to never again raise your voice
at those who would have understood your words
if you did not bear your culture, if you donned a different face.

to be a terrible, inconceivable, stunning
woman, and live.

LOVE LANGUAGE

1. once, the only word i knew in english was *maybe.*
i was taught early that the world is not black and white.
learn this word first.
let it flow into you, let it soften you.

2. childhood is a distant song i'll always sing along to.
love is a language that ripples through the past.
sometimes, i forget that once my arms were not arms
but a field of carnations.
i tell myself it's different now.

3. the librarian in the elementary school asks
what's your name? i reply *maybe.*
and the room bursts into laughter.
what did she say? look at this. the new girl's stupid.

4. years later, a long shadow hovers
above the cold slab of my body. my body,
wilting at the edges, the way auntie looked inside the box.
i say *no.* and he continues
to examine me with the eyes of a surgeon,
finding the exact place to cut so the hurt hardens upright.

5. i am not a broken girl. i know where my pieces lie,
each one, still mine. but men who love broken girls
always find me. first,
a ghost who took my legs when i was sleeping. second,
a boy with a kind sister who slit me down my fishbelly
and stuffed me full of pebbles. third,
a quiet burn who boiled flesh till it slid right off the bone.

fourth, a mask slowly filling with sand
until it tore off and took the sides of his face with it.

6. sweet girl, have you changed?
you say you stopped hurting yourself,
yet run towards men who do it for you.

7. i learned quickly that speaking with a new tongue takes practice.
fifteen minutes before the bell rings,
i prop open the back door of the library with a crayon.
i tiptoe in when the lights are off and hide between the shelves.
i touch each page, pronounce each word, remember each line.
one day, i'll be the one telling these stories.

8. language is what you train yourself to endure.

9. *what's your name?*
a mouthful of carnations, a voice
intent on beginning in place of a wound.

Heidi Wong is a poet and artist who grew up between Beijing, Hong Kong, and New York.

Specializing in expressionistic oil painting and hyper-realistic digital art, Heidi packs her poetry with equal intensity. Since first posting her work on social media at fifteen years old, she has developed a unique voice composed of the stark juxtaposition between surreal and macabre imagery and intimate and beautiful language.

NOTES

- Epigraph: *The Things They Carried* by Tim O'Brien
- goodbye to all that: Inspired by Joan Didion and Robert Graves
- what we gave each other: References "The Second Coming" by William Butler Yeats
- to the gods who do nothing:
  - "Come, let us go, and make thy father blind." – *Titus Andronicus* by William Shakespeare
  - "We will mourn with thee. O, could our mourning ease thy misery." – *Titus Andronicus* by William Shakespeare
  - "lay your hands on her, make her well, let her live." – References Mark 5:23
- lavinia does not die and instead becomes a poet:
  - "Fair Philomela, why, she but lost her tongue." – *Titus Andronicus* by William Shakespeare
- our story told in the wrong order:
  - "For stony limits cannot hold love out, And what love can do, that dares love attempt." – *Romeo and Juliet* by William Shakespeare
- extract this soft feeling: References "Spinster" by Sylvia Plath
- the inability to express oneself due to the inadequacy of language:
  - "What shall Cordelia speak? Love, and be silent." – *King Lear* by William Shakespeare
- for henry:
  - "At dawn she takes leave of the Yellow River, in the evening she arrives at Black Mountain." – *Ballad of Mulan* by Author Unknown